I Am Fair

Mary Elizabeth Salzmann

Consulting Editor, Monica Marx, M.A./Reading Specialist

ABDO
Publishing Company

Published by SandCastle™, an imprint of ABDO Publishing Company, 4940 Viking Drive, Edina, Minnesota 55435.

Printed in the United States.

Credits
Edited by: Pam Price
Curriculum Coordinator: Nancy Tuminelly
Cover and Interior Design and Production: Mighty Media
Photo Credits: Corbis Images, Digital Vision, Eyewire Images, PhotoDisc, Stockbyte

Library of Congress Cataloging-in-Publication Data

Salzmann, Mary Elizabeth, 1968-
    I am fair / Mary Elizabeth Salzmann.
       p. cm. -- (Building character)
    Includes index.
    Summary: Describes some of the many ways of being fair, including taking turns, following the rules, and including others in activities.
    ISBN 1-57765-826-4
    1. Fairness--Juvenile literature. [1. Fairness.] I. Title.

BJ1533.F2 S25 2002
179'.9--dc21
                                                                        2002066405

SandCastle™ books are created by a professional team of educators, reading specialists, and content developers around five essential components that include phonemic awareness, phonics, vocabulary, text comprehension, and fluency. All books are written, reviewed, and leveled for guided reading, early intervention reading, and Accelerated Reader® programs and designed for use in shared, guided, and independent reading and writing activities to support a balanced approach to literacy instruction.

Let Us Know

After reading the book, SandCastle would like you to tell us your stories about reading. What is your favorite page? Was there something hard that you needed help with? Share the ups and downs of learning to read. We want to hear from you! To get posted on the ABDO Publishing Company Web site, send us email at:

sandcastle@abdopub.com

SandCastle Level: Transitional

Your character is the kind of person you are.

You show your character in the things you say and do.

Fairness is part of your character.

I try to be fair.

There are many ways to be fair.

Being fair means sharing.

I share my treat with my sister.

When we take turns playing on the swing, we are being fair.

Including others is a good way to be fair.

We let everyone play our game.

When I invite all my friends
to my party, I am being fair.

Being fair means following
the rules.

I don't cheat at games.

It is fair to wait your turn.

I stay in my place in line.

Being fair means treating all people the same.

I pour the same amount in each glass.

What do you do to be fair?

Index

Glossary

amount how much of something there is

game an activity that has rules and that people do to have fun

line a row of people

party an event where people meet to have fun together

rules instructions that tell you what you should and should not do

swing a seat that hangs from chains or ropes that you can move back and forth on

About SandCastle™

A professional team of educators, reading specialists, and content developers created the SandCastle™ series to support young readers as they develop reading skills and strategies and increase their general knowledge. The SandCastle™ series has four levels that correspond to early literacy development in young children. The levels are provided to help teachers and parents select the appropriate books for young readers.

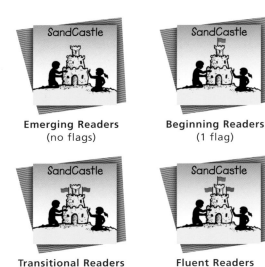

Emerging Readers
(no flags)

Beginning Readers
(1 flag)

Transitional Readers
(2 flags)

Fluent Readers
(3 flags)

These levels are meant only as a guide. All levels are subject to change.

To see a complete list of SandCastle™ books and other nonfiction titles from ABDO Publishing Company, visit www.abdopub.com or contact us at:

4940 Viking Drive, Edina, Minnesota 55435 • 1-800-800-1312 • fax: 1-952-831-1632